Oh My, Mammals!

Candice Ransom

Lerner Publications ◆ Minneapolis

Lerner Publications Company
An imprint of Lerner Publishing Group, Inc.
241 First Avenue North
Minneapolis, MN 55401 USA

For reading levels and more information, look up this title at www.lernerbooks.com.

Main body text set in Billy Infant Regular. Typeface provided by SparkyType.

Editor: Annie Zheng **Photo Editor:** Elena Mai

Library of Congress Cataloging-in-Publication Data

Names: Ransom, Candice F., 1952- author.
Title: Oh my, mammals! / Candice Ransom.
Description: Minneapolis, MN : Lerner Publications, [2026] | Series: Lightning bolt books. creepy creatures | Includes bibliographical references and index. | Audience: Ages 6-9 | Audience: Grades 2-3 | Summary: "Some mammals look cute, and others look creepy. Discover some of the world's strangest mammals from the star-nosed mole with its twenty-two fleshy feelers to wild babirusas that bare their sharp tusks"— Provided by publisher.
Identifiers: LCCN 2024037441 (print) | LCCN 2024037442 (ebook) | ISBN 9798765669013 (lib. bdg.) | ISBN 9798765684627 (pbk.) | ISBN 9798765679777 (epub)
Subjects: LCSH: Mammals—Juvenile literature.
Classification: LCC QL706.2 .R36 2026 (print) | LCC QL706.2 (ebook) | DDC 599—dc23/eng/20240911

LC record available at https://lccn.loc.gov/2024037441
LC ebook record available at https://lccn.loc.gov/2024037442

Manufactured in the United States of America
1-1011580-53872-11/12/2024

Table of Contents

Giant Freaky Bat

It is midnight in an African forest. A huge bat flaps to a fig tree.

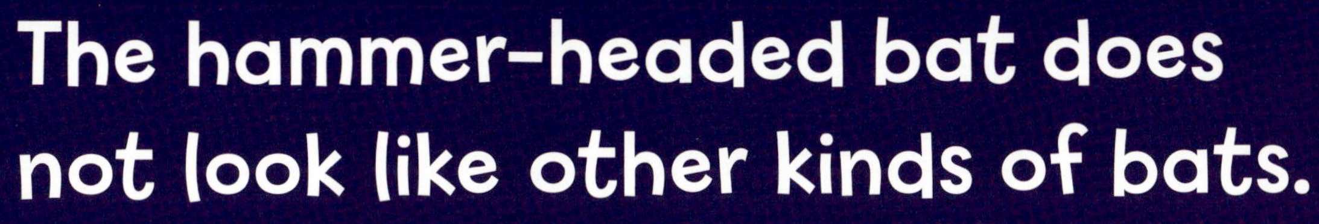

The hammer-headed bat does not look like other kinds of bats. Its head looks like a moose's head, with twisted lips.

Female hammer-headed bats have smaller heads than males.

Bats are mammals. Mammals are warm-blooded animals. They keep a certain body temperature.

Bats may seem scary. But most bats are harmless to people. **What are some other spooky mammals?**

People releasing rescued bats into the wild

Strange Mammals

The Tasmanian devil looks like a small dog. It is a marsupial. The females carry their young in a pouch.

Tasmanian devils are scavengers. This means they eat dead animals. A group of devils will fight over food. They show their sharp teeth and scream.

A Tasmanian devil screaming

The star-nosed mole has an unusual nose. Twenty-two fleshy feelers fan out from its nose. Those feelers allow the mole to find food.

Star-nosed moles cannot see well.

These moles use their front legs to dig tunnels.

The mole can sense a worm and eat it in less than a second. It is the fastest food hunter in the world. Its amazing nose can even smell insects underwater!

A tarsier leaps from tree to tree in the rainforest. This tiny primate has enormous eyes that let it see in the dark. It is the only primate that is a carnivore.

A tarsier's eye is roughly the size of its brain.

A tarsier leaping to catch a grasshopper

Its legs are longer than its body. Tarsiers can jump 10 feet (3.5 m) from tree to tree. They grip branches with special pads on their long fingers and toes.

The babirusa lives on an island in Indonesia. Male babirusas have four tusks. The tusks curl back over the animal's head.

Babirusa means "pig deer" in Malay.

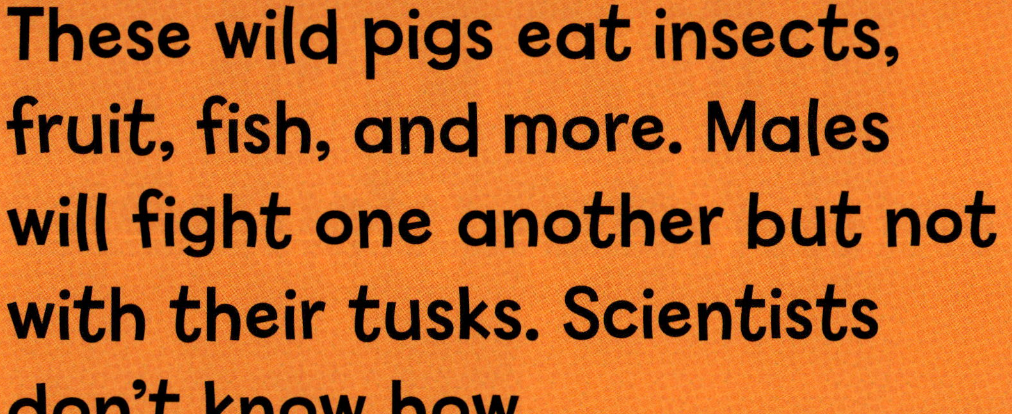

These wild pigs eat insects, fruit, fish, and more. Males will fight one another but not with their tusks. Scientists don't know how babirusas use their long, sharp tusks.

Their tusks are easily broken.

Different and Creepy

Mammals can be large like lions or small like shrews. Some mammals are cute. Others look scary.

Many people don't like strange-looking animals. They think these animals may cause them harm.

Pangolins are friendly animals.

A teen with their dog

People often prefer mammals that have big eyes and soft fur. Dogs and cats bring people comfort. Others, such as tigers and cheetahs, are cool.

Mammals are found all over our world. Most are harmless to humans. They grow, find food, and live peacefully with nature.

A red fox sniffing daisies

Spooky or Cute?

The aye-aye has big ears, round eyes, and bony fingers with claws. Its hair stands up when it is scared. Some people think this mammal looks spooky. Others think it has a cute face. Spooky or cute? What do you think?

Mammal Facts

- Humans are primates. You are a mammal!
- The largest mammal in the world is the blue whale.
- The cheetah is the fastest mammal on land. It can run 70 miles (113 km) per hour!
- No two zebras have the same stripe patterns.

Glossary

carnivore: an animal that eats other animals to live

fleshy: having a lot of flesh or fat

mammal: a warm-blooded animal that breathes air, has a backbone, and has hair at some time in its life

marsupial: a group of mammals that carry their young in a pouch

primate: a group of mammals that includes humans, apes, monkeys, tarsiers, and lemurs

shrew: a small mammal related to moles

tusk: a large tooth that sticks out of an animal's mouth

warm-blooded: able to keep a constant body temperature whether it is cold or hot outside

Learn More

Hansen, Grace. *How Mammals Evolved*. Minneapolis: Pop!, 2023.

Mattern, Joanne. *What's So Scary About Bats?* South Egremont, MA: Red Chair, 2023.

National Geographic Kids: Mammals
https://kids.nationalgeographic.com/animals/mammals

National Geographic Kids: Ooey Gooey Creepy Crawlies
https://kids.nationalgeographic.com/nature/article/ooey-gooey-creepy-crawlies-

Parrott-Ryan, Maria. *Mysterious Glowing Mammals: An Unexpected Discovery Sparks a Scientific Investigation*. Minneapolis: Millbrook Press, 2024.

San Diego Zoo Wildlife Explorers: Tasmanian Devil
https://sdzwildlifeexplorers.org/animals/tasmanian-devil

Index

Photo Acknowledgments

Image credits: MerlinTuttle.org/Science Source, p. 4; Ivan Kuzmin/Alamy, p. 5; Johner Images/Getty Images, p. 6; Mykola Miakshykov/Ukrinform/Future Publishing via Getty Images, p. 7; Daphne ROCHE/Getty Images, p. 8; JohnCarnemolla/Getty Images, p. 9; Adisha Pramod/Alamy, p. 10; Stan Tekiela Author/Naturalist/Wildlife Photographer/Getty Images, p. 11; Ignacio Palacios/Getty Images, p. 12; Jurgen Freund/Nature Picture Library/Alamy, p. 13; Riza Marlon/Getty Images, p. 14; Gerard Lacz/mauritius images GmbH/Alamy, p. 15; Life on white/Alamy, p. 16; Imagevixen/RooM the Agency/Alamy, p. 17; Jessie Casson/Getty Images, p. 18; Johnny Johnson/Getty Images, p. 19; Ellen Goff/Danita Delimont/Alamy, p. 20.

Cover: holgs/Getty Images.